I
Saw
GOD

...in the midst of tragedy

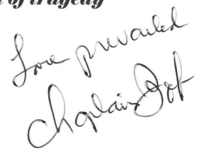

Love prevailed

Chaplain Bob

Bobj @ NTeLos. NeT

540 292 9100

I
Saw
GOD

...in the midst of tragedy

A Chaplain's Experience at Ground Zero

By Bob Johnson

Bob Johnson Ministries, LLC
Waynesboro, VA

I Saw God ...*in the midst of tragedy*
A Chaplain's Experience at Ground Zero

Copyright © 2008 by Bob Johnson Ministries, LLC

ISBN: 978-0-9778439-1-6

Additional copies are also available on the World Wide Web at
www.chaplainbobwtcministry.com

Cover design by Theresa Dexter, Tdexter13@aol.com
Typesetting and print production by ePlus Solutions, print@e-plussolutions.com

This book is written in memory of

The Fire personnel,
Police officers,
Public workers,
And civilians

Who gave their lives to rescue others.

*

Also in memory of
Roland Kandle, Commander

*

This book is dedicated to the families of
Those who died on that fateful day.

*

This book is also dedicated to
The ones who risked their lives to
See others live.

*

I also dedicate this book to the many
Chaplains who served at
The site of the WTC disaster.

Acknowledgements

My heartfelt thanks and appreciation go to many named and unnamed individuals and organizations. Without their encouragement and support, this book would not have been written.

I send an extra expression of thanks:

To the International Conference of Police Chaplains, who gave me the opportunity to serve at the site of the World Trade Center disaster and provided the training necessary to become a disaster Chaplain.

To the Staunton Police Department, who gave me the honor of serving as their chaplain. Without their endorsement, I could not have been part of the ICPC.

To Mt. Zion-Linville Church of the Brethren, for their support of time and money, without which my trip could not have been possible, and for the letters and encouragement they sent to the heroes.

To Travis Simmons for his inspiration and thoughts.

To those who generously gave me gifts of appreciation during my service in New York. The tie tack, stuffed bear, hard hat, Red Cross chaplain's vest, countless pins and picture of the World Trade Center towers signed by dozens of volunteers and agency workers are among my most treasured possessions.

To my editor, Cheryl Lewis, who took my experiences after 9/11 and wove luster and life into their description.

To my lovely wife, Linda Gail. Without her love, support and sacrifice, I would not have had the opportunity to serve.

Thank you all!

Contents

Preface

Hate takes many forms. On 9/11, it wore the face of fanatical delusion as terrorists united to destroy thousands of innocent lives in New York City. That day, our nation and countless lives were forever altered. Grieving took the place of vitality and suffering replaced industry. In the chasm left where soaring skyscrapers had stood, an entire nation was crushed.

Or so the terrorists had hoped.

And then God began to remind the world, in ways seen and unseen, heralded and private, trumpeted and whispered, that He never, ever leaves our side. In one tragic instant, the hearts and minds of Americans and others around the world shifted from our own ambitions, worries and rat race. As a horrified global community watched the devastation unfolding in one of the world's most bustling and heavily populated cities, an outpouring of love and compassion and offers to help immediately followed.

Within hours, teams were mobilizing in thousands of communities to send physical and financial aid. Rescuers began desperate searches, at their own peril, to unearth and attempt to save the fallen. Many individuals, including dozens of firefighters and rescue personnel, died as a result of their selflessness.

Among them was Father Mychal Judge, who was administering last rites to a victim at Ground Zero when he, too, lost his life.

I didn't know this chaplain personally, but his death moved me deeply. Would I be willing to give my life as he had done? Could I risk losing everything I'd spent my lifetime to gain?

As I considered this haunting question and thought of my colleagues, the answer became clear to me. Yes, I knew in my heart they would all respond with the same compassion and courage. My yearning to go and help convinced me that I, too, would give whatever God asked of me.

Questioning God's presence during a time of loss is tempting.

I'm a man of faith and even I felt tormented by the heartache of so many. But He showed His face to me and the world, again and again, through the lives and giving hearts of those who stood to serve where others had fallen.

He is among us. We just have to open our eyes and see.

This book is my attempt to share what He showed me.

Chapter One
✠
An Unforgettable Day

It was just another day. I was sitting in the Waffle Inn, one of my favorite restaurants, getting ready to order a mid-morning breakfast, when the waitress appeared with a strange look on her face. Frozen by our table, her coffee pot in hand, she never uttered a word nor filled our cups.

"What's wrong?" I asked, alarmed.

Her response made no sense to me.

"A plane just hit a large building in New York City, and thousands of people are dead."

Surely she was mistaken. But then I heard the feverish newscasts now being turned up on the diner's radio. Every ear in the place heard the shocking news: the World Trade Center was engulfed in flames and scores of people were undoubtedly dead.

The restaurant's patrons sat in stunned silence. The calm that generally reflected our fair town's natural peace and quiet was replaced by a growing sense of horror by all present. This was no simple tragedy. This was big - profoundly, terribly big.

We couldn't know it, but what was happening before us would set a new global benchmark for heartache and loss.

As I drove home in a numbed daze, I couldn't imagine

that the worst horrors were yet ahead.

But it was so. As I rushed inside to check telecasts on the disaster, I watched with fresh disbelief at footage of the second airliner colliding with the second tower in New York City. It just couldn't be.

Then, with the rest of America and, indeed, the world, I saw each of the World Trade Center towers begin to collapse in upon themselves until nothing was left but flames, hysteria and rubble. Reeling, I realized I had just witnessed more than 3,000 people perishing in about 30 seconds.

It was too awful to grasp.

Who could have caused such a thing? What evil could possess a person or group to commit such a heinous act?

And, perhaps most importantly, *where was God?*

That's not a question that a pastor typically asks. In fact, since I was a child, I had never questioned whether God was near. It just always seemed clear to me that we were a team. But how could the loving God that I knew allow such atrocity?

I felt certain I wasn't the only one to wonder. I was also convinced, like so many others, that I needed to help. Perhaps it was my way of getting closer to the answer to my own perplexing question. Maybe I just needed to be near to those who were hurting in hopes of easing some of the pain that I had inexplicably escaped.

One thing was for sure - I was sitting in my living room and, above all else, I knew I needed to head *home.*

Chapter Two

✝

Home Is Where Memories Live

I'm no longer young. The years have flown and, what do you know, here I am, on the other side of the age spectrum. But that doesn't change the fact that we always feel youthful inside, does it? I can remember, like it was yesterday, the chaos of my youth with horns honking and people bustling and smells of hot dogs on street carts and, oh, the taste of a roast beef hero, with an extra dose of mayonnaise and potato salad! Those memories will always be New York City to me. I was born and raised on Long Island and New York City, in all of its overwhelming, vast, fast-paced frenzy, will forever be familiar and dear.

Of course, just because you are raised near the city doesn't mean what most people imagine. Long Island was country. We had hunting and fishing and horseback riding and golf. Sure, the houses were close together, but only like what you would think of in a town. When I was a teen, I would go into the city with friends of mine. We would take the train and see shows and look around and see the Empire State Building. It was just around the corner, geographically speaking, but the pace of living there was different enough from what we experienced on an average day that we savored the excitement.

When I was entering my twenties, I grabbed hold of the chance for adventure and took a job driving a bus in the city. Can you imagine? Most people would never dream of trying to drive there – and certainly not a huge charter bus! But I loved the challenge and found it exciting. The streets were narrow and had very close borders, so I had to squeeze during my turns onto each new block. It took a lot of skill to get through – and courage! People didn't care one bit about whether you were happy or sad or worried or lost – *beep beep hurry up*! I'd be driving along, trying to find something, and they'd be shouting for me to get out of their way! That might not sound friendly to you, but it was all part of the thrill of being part of something bigger than myself and I was having a blast. I will never forget the fun of finally finding where I was trying to go or managing to park once I got there. Imagine trying to park a bus in NYC!

Back then, it was a truly dangerous place. After a girl walking home during the wee hours one night was murdered, a van service was created to provide safe transportation to residents from 6 at night to 6 in the morning. I filled in, from time to time, for my brother driving that van's route. You had to be careful, because it was seriously dangerous. It wasn't like it is today, now that the city has been cleaned up a good bit. But always, along with the danger, there was the heightened sense that NYC was an exciting place to be. Just to peer up at the endless skyscrapers and explore Broadway and Times Square and Radio City Music Hall and gobble up food from the street vendors was a thrill.

Those memories never quite leave you.

Still, time passes. I got older and moved on from the

frenzied pace of city living and wound up in one of the most quaint, quiet communities you can imagine. Shenendoah Valley is an idyllic area of Virginia and the church I pastor there is filled with loving, caring and peaceful hearts. Life, for me, was quiet and full.

And then came 9/11.

While I sat in that breakfast nook in Verona, hundreds of miles away from the bustle of New York City, and heard of the devastation occurring near my hometown, all of the sensations of my youth came crashing in and I needed, more than anything else, to be near to those who were scrambling to survive and, later, to recover. I needed to see for myself what had changed in my beloved city and to reach out to those who were hurting and let them know that I was there if they needed me. They weren't alone. Despite the horrors of what evil had unleashed, God was with them and hope was not lost.

My wish to rush to the side of those in need was not immediately granted. Like so much of my life, I had to do my best to put the wheels in motion, trust God's plan and then trust that He would lead me to the place where He needed me most.

I hadn't always been a pastor, you see. When I was growing up, I always felt God had something for me to do, so I expressed my desire to enter the Lutheran church's ranks. I discovered, to my dismay, that the priesthood would include learning a formidable amount of Latin. I was still young and, let me tell you, spending my days and nights in the books of a language few still spoke did not appeal to me.

My career path, instead, veered to the trucking

industry. Many years later, I was asked by a friend to join the police reserves and, since it was a realm where I felt I could serve others, I enthusiastically agreed. Still, I stayed close to the church and was generally immersed in its activities. So, when I was asked as a reserve officer to become a volunteer police chaplain, it seemed providence was steering me toward a role of dual service that I could savor. Each time I mentioned wanting to become a pastor, it seemed a new opportunity to serve others as a law enforcement chaplain opened up.

Finally, God steered me toward a small congregation that needed someone to serve as pastor. I was honored by their invitation and felt humbled to look back at the path that God had drawn to their door. I knew I was at the right place just when I was needed most.

When the crisis gripped New York City and the nation continued to watch in rapt horror, I had to remind myself again and again that God's timing is not always my own. I agonized over the delays that were stalling my urgent desire to help. I had called the home office of the International Conference of Police Chaplains (ICPC) and had my name added to the list of chaplains willing to serve. Because I had been informed that response teams were being deployed, but advised not to respond until I was called, I tried waiting impatiently for a couple of weeks. My next call assured me I was on the list to go in October but, as the end of October neared, I called again and learned it would be November - but I was first on the list.

Each day that passed, I thought of the unspeakable heartache that must surely be burdening the families of victims and the anguish of those who had survived. I knew the rescue teams and volunteers would be weathering extreme fatigue and discouragement and that grief was blanketing an entire nation. I had nothing I could truly offer them – except the enduring belief that what is impossible for men is possible with God; that sharing His love and compassion could ease the deepest hurt; that my shoulder was strong enough for someone to lean on and my ear was ready to listen to any who needed to talk. I wanted to offer what God had given me and I prayed that my chance would come soon.

In November, when my assignment was received at last, I rejoiced. Yes, the knowledge that I was responding to a major catastrophe delivered through evil was sobering and my mind raced with the unknown. I didn't have a clue what to expect or what lay ahead. But I have a big God and knew great healing can happen through those who honor Him. All I could do was step forward and say, "Here am I, Lord. Use me as You will."

Chapter Three
☦
A Call To Action

God blessed me with a wonderful wife. Not only is Gail a talented professional, but she is a caring woman and one who supports me unconditionally. It couldn't have been easy for her to see me off that November morning as I left for what we both knew would be a heart-wrenching duty. But we consoled ourselves in the knowledge that my absence would only stretch across a few weeks. Those I would be seeking to comfort had no such luxury.

So it was with heavy hearts but appreciation for God's blessings in our own lives that we made our way to the Amtrak station. Thanks to their generosity, I traveled without charge to my destination. That might seem a small matter to many, but I saw God in that simple accommodation. Anything that could ease worry at such a difficult time was welcomed with humble gratitude.

The kindness demonstrated by Amtrak was the first of many thoughtful acts that I would savor in the difficult days to come. In fact, as I arrived at New Jersey Penn, I was awestruck by the news that two out-of-state law-enforcement officers would soon pick me up. From across the nation, selfless officers had offered their services to transport the many chaplains and critical-stress teams to locations around the city. As I mentioned before, it's not exactly the easiest place in which to drive – especially if you're not familiar with the intricacies of traffic! These were heroes, indeed.

It was very cold in New Jersey that night and, as I waited for the officers to arrive, I wished for a warm place to huddle. A local police officer who was on duty at Penn Station saw me standing outside and offered me a seat in his patrol car. Again, I saw God in this simple act of unsolicited kindness. The warmth he shared as I waited for the unknown stretched beyond my toes and into my aching heart.

When two officers from Boston arrived, I had no idea that we were about to embark on a mini-adventure of our own. Since none of us were familiar with the route before us, we puzzled over directions and seemed to get lost – many, many times. You can imagine that New York's metro area is not exactly where you'd like to be floundering.

As we drove around in circles, one officer would look at the other and ask, "Do you know where we are?" and the other would respond, "No, do you?" Despite the grim disaster that had inspired us all to become part of the massive volunteer team, we found ourselves immersed in laughter. Their humor eased my transition into a difficult environment in a way that little else could have accomplished.

At last, we arrived at the Command Center at Journal Square and, after going through the National Guard's meticulous security checkpoints, I met my commander. With a stern face, salt-and-pepper hair and a no-nonsense manner, Roland Kandle made it clear in no uncertain terms that there would be no hand holding during our volunteer stint. I decided my best course of action would be to become a great listener and keep my mouth shut. It was abundantly clear that it was "his way or the highway" and, after all I'd gone through to participate in the first place, I wasn't about to get sent home.

Roland's credentials were convincing. The leader of the New Jersey Critical Incident Stress Management Team, he was also a Vietnam veteran. He was a certified fire marshal and had a degree in fire science. A specialist in fire prevention, he was a former fire chief in Elmer, New Jersey. We're talking one tough guy. But, extremely active in organizing fundraisers for burn foundations, Roland's gruff exterior and sharp voice were only a cover for his big heart.

The evening was rather whirl wind. Heavily secured in the Port Authority Police Building in Jersey City, we toured the facilities and then enjoyed a delicious meal – that was also free. Again, the generosity of others created comfort for us and I was grateful.

When I learned I would be sharing a hotel room with three other chaplains, I began to wonder if my comfort was coming to an end. Sure, I knew we'd need to bunk together to reduce costs and get to know one another, but I had no idea what to expect since predicting others' personalities is a bit of a wild card.

In reality, it was a real delight to meet three other men from different backgrounds and scattered ends of the country working together for a common purpose. After beginning the day with lots of questions and few answers, traveling many hundreds of miles, having an adventuresome ride, meeting my commander and new roommates, I felt certain that I was exactly where God intended me to be. I just had to keep trusting Him and His plan.

As it turned out, the three other compassionate men with whom I would share a room had made the same journey from around the country: California, Indiana and me from New York by way of Virginia. We were quite a mix, I must say.

Ray was an experienced chaplain who had already served in October, but was back to guide us rookies with lots of fervor and wisdom. He put us at ease and shared his expertise, It was clear he loved what he was doing. I saw God in this gentle man who was so willing to lead others in a selfless way.

At that first day's end, I thanked God for the privilege of experiencing everything that one day had held. I had traveled safely and seen the thoughtfulness of others. My heart was expanding to include those He'd brought into my world.

My appreciation for those already dear to me was deepening as well. Perhaps the knowledge that I would soon be facing the stark loss of so many families made me pensive but, even after only one afternoon, I missed being with my wife.

Still, I knew my yearning was nothing compared to the devastation being felt that very moment by thousands of husbands and wives and children and parents just these few short weeks after 9/11. My prayer that evening included us all.

Chapter Four

✝

Day One

It seemed fitting somehow that the first morning I awoke as part of the official crisis volunteer effort was Veterans Day. Somewhere, as I tugged on my boots and prepared for a day of comforting victims and families of 9/11, there were other young men and women facing the certain challenges that the new fight against terror would introduce. Around the world were others who had served during past crises. They were all in my thoughts as the other chaplains and I readied ourselves for the day and headed back to the Command Center for assignments.

By now, our stomachs were churning and we couldn't make out whether it was hunger or just nerves. When we opened the door and joined the hubbub, the heavenly aroma of coffee and frying bacon wrapped around my senses. Have you ever seen God in a stack of hotcakes? I did that morning. It was just the boost I needed to face what I knew would likely be a traumatic day.

I was surrounded by others who had come to serve. Police officers, Critical Incident Stress Management Team members, deputy sheriffs and even a K-9 dog gathered near to learn how they could best help others. They had trekked from far and near to meet the needs of those who were piecing together the shreds that terrorism had caused. Their unselfish attitudes were refreshing and inspirational. As I watched each of them step forward to tackle whatever task was needed, I vowed to do the same.

After receiving our procedural ground rules, which needed to be followed to the letter, we were given our assignments. I would be heading to the World Trade Center site and Pier 94. The core of the devastation, Ground Zero was known to these volunteers as Ground Hero, instead. To further inspire this train of thinking, a good-natured rule in our ranks mandated that anyone slipping up and using the wrong moniker was required to add a dollar to the Family of Victims fund.

Our roles for the day were set and, barring unforeseen circumstances, everything would be orderly.

In New York City, unforeseen circumstances were becoming commonplace.

Before we could depart for our scheduled assignments, the television delivered more stunning news: an airliner had crashed on Long Island and untold lives had surely been lost.

What had seemed a straightforward day of tending to those we would meet at our assigned sites was instantly thrown into tumult. An intensive security alert was enacted as New York City was again shut down. No one could be certain whether this crash was the act of terrorists and all activities were frozen until details could be sorted out.

We all listened, watched and waited apprehensively, expressing our deep sorrow for the victims on that plane and the many families their loss would impact. A sense of helplessness seized us all, since we were locked down at the

Command Center – ready to help but unauthorized to act.

There are many times when we encounter that feeling in daily living, aren't there? We may feel a yearning to serve and yet not quite know how to be of service or who to help. So we stand in place, keeping an eye open for opportunity and heart ready for action – and wait. It can be a frustrating feeling.

On this day, several hours of relentless anxiety passed before an "all clear" signal was delivered. Most of the day had passed and the atmosphere of uncertainty had intensified. But my determination to comfort those who were hurting had also grown. I knew that there were people out there who would need a caring heart and compassionate shoulder upon which they could lean. They needed to know, in the midst of so much horror, that God is still profoundly present.

Once the security alert was eased, we were routed to our various site assignments. My group and I were delivered to Pier 94. All of the different agencies – Red Cross, Salvation Army, many insurance agencies, state agencies, health agencies and the like – were stationed there to help those who had lost loved ones. It was moving to be in the midst of hundreds of people who were sharing in one common cause: to help those who were hurting.

As I looked out on this vast array of people and the agencies they represented, I saw God. He was in the people who were helping others cope with this disaster. He was touching lives through those who cared enough to help the families of the slain. It no longer mattered where someone was raised or whether they had money or if the color of their skin matched the neighbor's. It was one united team of humanity.

As I made my way through the masses of people and agencies, set up in rows as far as the eye could see, I met a retired police officer from New York whose brother had been killed in the North Tower's collapse. He shared with me quietly about how his brother had insisted on going back inside in hope of tugging others free of the debris after the building's collapse. That was the last time he was seen alive.

It was clear this man's heart was breaking to have lost one so dear. But his pride in his brother's profound sacrifice and selfless nature was also evident. I saw God in his tear-filled eyes.

It was then that I knew my reason to have come so far, with no certainty that my presence could benefit others, was to listen. My ministry would be one of presence. I couldn't fix what these people were going through – no human could. But I could give them everything in me so that they could share their grief and see, intimately, that someone cares and is willing to share their pain.

I wanted them to see God in me.

As I lifted my prayers after our conversation for this man and his family, I came upon another man. He was sitting in a wheelchair and shared that he'd been inside the World Trade Center as it burned. In his quest that fateful day to make his way from the fourth floor below ground, he had opened a door that blew back in his face and propelled him over a table. When he had revived, he was filled with horror at the sight and pain of his severely disfigured leg.

I wanted to cry out, too, at the pain I saw in his face, but tried to focus instead on his need to be heard.

On 9/11, he was one of the fortunate few who heard

a voice in the darkness, calling out to anyone who might need aid. As they stumbled toward each other, these two men realized they would have to find an exit quickly – or die. After literally crawling up four flights of stairs – which seemed to take hours – they joyously made it to safety against horrific odds.

As I listened to his story of triumph and experienced his lingering grief over losing so many, I knew God was present in his face. Such fortitude and perseverance is a genuine gift from above and one we can all access if only we are willing. I felt awed by this man who had not given up.

He was not alone.

That afternoon, I met another gentleman who was steering those needing services to the appropriate agency locations. As we chatted, he shared that he was a survivor of the 1993 attack on the World Trade Center. He had lost a leg in that bombing. Feeling blessed to simply be alive, he was now dedicating his days to helping others find comfort and assistance. He didn't want anyone wondering whether they were surrounded by a caring nation, full of love and compassion.

Could anyone doubt that God's presence was in this place?

I would soon find out. As the day advanced, my assignment shifted from Pier 94 to the actual scene of September's unspeakable horror and destruction – the World Trade Center site. Now called "the Pit" by those who worked in its depths, Ground Hero was the place I felt I would likely be needed the most.

It had been less than two months since the terrorist attacks and the horror there was still palpable. The piles of rubble from two massive towers of steel and their contents lay collapsed like twisted mountains of despair. Heaping four stories high in some areas, the destruction reduced me to absolute silence. Fires were still burning and smoke billowed out from beneath the surface. The smells were wretched.

Knowing I was standing at the gravesite of 3,000 innocent people who were murdered to satisfy hate, I felt nausea and grief churn within me.

I knew there was nothing I could do or say alone to help anyone here. I was in way over my head. The loss was just too great. Bowing my head, I said an earnest prayer begging God to use me to comfort others in this tragedy and to help me cope with whatever the day would present.

God heard me and, as I walked further into the Pit, a New York City police officer came over and asked me to meet with a man standing nearby. She explained that he was the brother of one of the victims who had perished. Not far away was a woman and two children – they had lost a husband and father through that same death.

After meeting with them to offer comfort, I was shaken and my eyes filled with tears. How could one family endure so much? Where was God?

And then I knew: God was there through me, allowing me to be an encouraging vessel to those who were hurting and to let them know we deeply care. He was also there in the compassionate attention of the group of firefighters who drew near, offering words of consolation and encouragement. Not only were they weathering their own grief over lost loved ones and comrades, they were working the site to help with the structural healing and thanking those around them for caring enough to come.

Strengthened by such unselfishness and sacrifice, I thanked God for continuing to answer my prayers and for showing me His face in the lives of so many.

During a visit to Fire Station Ten for a welcome rest and refreshment, again provided by precious volunteers, I went upstairs and was confronted by a view I will never forget. Before me were sprawled 16 acres of total destruction. Again, it reduced me to absolute silence and prayer – both for the lives needlessly lost and for those left behind to cope with wrenching heartache.

That evening, as I fell gratefully into my welcoming bed, I had a prayer of thanks on my lips – for those families He allowed me to comfort and for the people around me so willing to give.

Chapter Five
✟
A New Day

The new morning dawned and I was again assigned to the Pit. I wondered whose paths would cross mine and prayed that God would use me again to bring His love into the lives of many who were desperately hurting.

In order to accommodate families of victims and give them a place at which they could pay respect to loved ones who were lost, the city government had erected an overlook platform and I made my way there. Across the rear area, a large board was signed by many families and dignitaries who had visited. I signed my name just below the signature of President George W. Bush and felt honored to add my tribute to those who had paid homage.

As I turned to leave, I noticed a woman over in the corner sobbing. She was holding a mask over her face to quell the stench from the still-burning fires. After I introduced myself, she acknowledged that she had lost someone in the disaster. When I offered to pray for her, she acquiesced, adding, "I wish you would."

Following our brief prayer, she leaned forward and gently kissed me on the cheek, then walked over to the side of an older gentleman who was standing nearby. The two of them leaned on each other and then she assisted him down the steps.

For every person standing near the site, there was a story of loss – whether it was as family, neighbor, friend, co-worker or American. It was wrenching to feel their grief and soothing to share their prayer. I saw God each time the tension in their clenched jaws and stressed shoulders eased after they were given the space to share and be heard or simply to receive prayer.

On one occasion, I introduced myself to a firefighter who was taking a brief rest. Imagine our surprise when we discovered his son was playing football for my high school alma mater! It struck me that a conversation that would seem so ordinary in any other context took on extraordinary dimensions in the surreal setting of Ground Hero.

My first goal was to make myself emotionally and physically available to anyone who God might bring into my path and so I wandered a lot. When I wound up at St. Paul's Cathedral, I was struck by its majesty. Despite all odds, it remained standing when the towers collapsed beside it.

You could feel a sense of God's power just by looking at its soaring grandeur. You could also see Him in the hundreds of banners, flowers and pictures placed on every available surface in front of the church. He was evident in the faces of the people who gathered along the fence throughout each day and night to pray.

Inside, the church had been temporarily converted into a respite area where the site workers and volunteers could retreat for prayer and sustenance. The mere sight of the thousands of letters and pictures from all over the world that had been hung around the church's interior was enough to leave you speechless and prayerful.

Many were seated in quiet prayer and others simply sat in contemplation and stared through the beauty of the stain-glassed windows. Volunteer massage therapists offered healing hands to anyone needing relief from physical aches and ministers did the same for those seeking spiritual support.

Many workers had been in the field 12 to 16 hours and were ready to collapse when they reached the church. Yet they were willing to return and continue their search-and-recovery work even when already facing exhaustion. I saw God in their tired but determined shoulders.

I was asked, many times, as I trekked on my rounds, "Where was God on 9/11?" I could see that most of these individuals wanted an answer that would reassure them they had not been abandoned during a time of unspeakable tragedy. My response, again and again, was "Look around. He is here. He has always been here."

More than ever, I was certain that God was among us and truly had never left. There can be no simple answer to those who have experienced tragedy and want to know why. Sometimes what occurs in life is inexplicable. Evil exists in man. Yet God does not turn His face.

As I experienced the inner tenacity of relentless workers and saw the intense faith of the hundreds gathered in vigil outside the church, I saw Him time and again.

It was enough to keep restoring my tired spirit and, again, I thanked God for the privilege of serving alongside so many amazing individuals.

Chapter Six

✝

Flying High

I have a confession to make.

I've always had a bit of a taste for adventure. Indeed, when I was a few days younger than I am now (OK, so it was decades), I decided to tackle the challenge of greeting the world beneath the surface of our oceans. Yep, I wanted to become a scuba diver. I love the water and thought it would be a real challenge. I wasn't wrong! Just figuring out the tangle of gear seemed adventure enough for awhile there! I looked like a little Michelin man with my wet suit and gear on.

While my shallow dives in the local quarry were a big success, I wasn't thrilled when my weight belt fell around my knees during a deep dive and my fin came off. (Hint: Diving without a weight belt and fin is definitely not recommended!)

So I switched to flying. I could be a Master Ace, right up there alongside of Snoopy! It would be great to see how the world looks to God, right? Besides, it was practically doctor's orders.

"Take up a hobby to rest your mind from ministry," a dear friend had advised. I suspect he meant play bridge or learn Scrabble. But, no, safe was hardly my style!

Flying was a breeze (no pun intended) until it came to landing. Well, it is often said in pilot circles that "taking off is optional but landing is mandatory!" And my landings were not pretty. I won't tell you about the time I crashed and destroyed my instructor's plane, but you would assume that would have been enough to deter me – or him - but no!

It was not until I was later flying a twin-engine plane to Myrtle Beach that I met my comeuppance. As I simultaneously encountered a sudden wind shear and mountain wave – two of the worst turbulences you can encounter while airborne – I thought certain my end was near. I told God that if He wanted me to die I would, but I wasn't going to make it easy for Him. He must have laughed and said, "OK, Bob, I will see you through this but, remember, the third time might not be a charm!"

That was the end of my flyboy days.

Somehow, when I signed up to head to New York City to volunteer, in the back of my mind I was thinking it might also have the ingredients for an adventure. There is something about the unknown that can be stimulating – even as it is a bit fearsome.

So, yes, I wanted to genuinely and solemnly offer my heart to those who needed comforting after such profound loss. But it was tough to quell that inner instinct of mine that found the prospect of adventure so enticing. Who knew what I might see and experience?

I was not disappointed.

After my service at Ground Hero, I was assigned to the John F. Kennedy Airport. Only two days after Flight 587 had crashed at nearby Bell Harbor, Long Island, we were sent to comfort the Port Authority Police. They had lost

37 members of their force when the World Trade Center towers collapsed. Many of their homes and the homes of those who had died at Ground Zero were located in this very neighborhood. For these enduring individuals, loss seemed relentless.

Invited by an officer to tour the airport, I climbed enthusiastically into the huge fire equipment truck alongside her. One of the massive foam-and-water trucks that are called upon during fuel-spillage or fire crises, the truck was designed to get very close to fires and was amazing. I was thrilled to see how she expertly maneuvered it around the tarmac.

And then God gently reminded me why I was there.

As we drove, this brave woman shared with me that she had lost her partner just weeks before in the World Trade Center devastation. She was still traumatized and felt guilty for being the one who was now driving the truck – since that had been her partner's role. She talked, sharing how it seemed that death was all around her, and we rode. An hour passed as she spilled out her anguish and memories – then two hours had flown by.

Her story was deeply moving and I silently thanked God for giving me the ministry of presence. It felt good for me to listen and for her to feel heard. Neither of us had illusions that I could "fix" things nor even try to make sense of it all. She just needed someone to be willing to let her unload her burdens and to care.

While we were driving, we saw that the Concorde was open and she asked if I'd like to see inside.

Did I hear her right?

Was she seriously asking me, a chaplain with a pilot's

license and enthusiast from way back, if I wanted to see the flight deck of one of the greatest aircraft ever?

With permission from the security guard, we stepped aboard and I felt overwhelmed by the thrill of it all. The instrument panel was massive and I itched to sit in the pilot's chair. Boy, what would it be like to fly this baby? I imagined popping over to London for a quick visit – with me behind the controls, naturally. It would certainly be a far stretch from the Cherokee Piper I was used to flying at a top speed of 120 mph!

To some, that might not sound very exciting. But to an amateur pilot who has not even mastered instrument flying and, in fact, has only flown first class because a friend bought the ticket, standing in that cockpit was beyond wonderful. Had I sent a handwritten note to God requesting adventure during my somber stay in New York City, He could not have answered my secret hope more fully.

That bit of pleasure would have to hold me for the duration of the trip, because what lay just ahead would take all of the stamina I could muster.

Chapter Seven

✟

Flight 587

According to eyewitnesses, when Flight 587 plummeted into the ground on Long Island, it came straight down, spinning in a downward spiral, and then exploded upon impact. The devastation two days later, when I arrived for my assigned duties, covered two large blocks one block wide. Two homes had been destroyed and those living in one home were killed.

It was tough for many to see God's presence in this tragedy that came so soon after the neighboring horrors. But there was evidence that here, too, He was near.

Had the airliner descended downward at an angle, many more lives would surely have been lost. Indeed, if the engine had landed anywhere other than where it did, additional homes in the area would likely have been destroyed. Many residents had been protected from unspeakable loss.

I saw God in the firefighters and neighbors who were helping others to be calm and He was in the Red Cross workers who had set up a respite area so those who were affected could have refreshment and a place to rest.

There were numerous agencies on site: local police, firefighters, Red Cross, FBI, National Transportation Safety

Board, ICPC (International Conference of Police Chaplains), and the New York City mayor's office – all working together to help the victims and evaluate this tragic event.

God was present in the love and compassion shown to others by the staff and volunteers of these many agencies.

As I spoke with some of the neighbors about their experiences, a fire captain approached me and asked if I would bless the red bag she was holding – and then go with her to a nearby truck so I could bless the 27 red bags that were already tucked inside.

When I asked, a bit hesitantly, what the bags contained, I was stunned by her reply.

"These bags contain the body parts of people that have been recovered at the site," she quietly responded. "We'd like for you to say a prayer over them before they're taken away."

I had never done a service over a body part before. So I took a deep breath, asked God for His wisdom and presence, and moved with her toward the truck and its contents.

I offered a blessing in the name of God and then read the 23rd Psalm over each bag, closing with a brief prayer. I had no way of knowing the identity of this person or their faith, so I simply turned everything over to God to give peace to their family.

We spent the next several hours with a lieutenant of the FDNY placing body parts in red bags, and I continued to offer blessings over them. Because I didn't know the faith, if any, of the people who had perished, I offered simple prayers and trusted God to do the rest.

The day seemed to stretch on forever, wrapped in the

sharing of grief, stories of tragedy and loss of life. I confess that the stench of death and feeling of helplessness was overwhelming but, through it all, I felt God's presence and He strengthened me.

That evening, I fell into an exhausted sleep and, the next morning, we were again assigned the crash site of 587. It seemed Roland had received favorable reports of our participation there and he wanted us to continue.

Again designated to assist the fire captain, I spent the day waiting for the crew working the site to bring us the remains of victims of the crash. After the lieutenant and captain tried to find identification and tagged each bag, I offered blessings over the remains.

Soon after our second day's work began there, a fireman came out of the rubble carrying a small red bag. He was very upset and carefully handed the bag to the lieutenant. As she cautiously opened it, we looked in and saw the remains of a small child.

This was a very traumatic moment for us all.

Standing in mutual shock and distress, we hugged each other as tears flowed down our faces. The demands of the tasks at hand forced us to compose ourselves and return to our duties, but we were all shaken and stricken with fresh grief.

It was profoundly moving to see the professionalism and genuine care taken by these firefighters to ensure respect was given to this little child and the others whose lives were ended by this tragic crash.

The blessing ritual was never once overlooked and I felt renewed to work with individuals who demonstrated such concern for life and compassion when confronted by its loss.

Such work was grueling and emotional and the Red Cross volunteers who kept us continually plied with refreshments were a godsend. I remember one in particular. She was one of the shortest, sweetest ladies I've ever met.

What impressed me most about this shorter-than-me (tough to achieve!) person was her smile. It was contagious. It brightened up the whole area and made my day. After seeing the most gruesome sights and continually having my emotions tested, I needed that smile.

Her personality was wonderful as well. She was just full of fun and hugs and I felt special around her. She couldn't do enough to help and she provided mind-soothing thoughts in a place that had none. We had only spoken for about five minutes when, all of a sudden, she came over and simply hugged me again and told me how proud she was of me and thanked me for the work I was doing.

That moment was emotional for me because it was clear, once again, that God was present in her sunny attitude. Despite grim surroundings, she was determined to spread cheer and it had a restorative effect on my psyche. After my coffee break, I returned to work and my step was lighter because of her impact.

Not long after, I encountered several Jewish youths who had witnessed the crash. They shared their heart-wrenching tale and the fear was evident in their faces as they contemplated the difference the plane's descent angle had made in their own futures. The school they had been attending at the time of the crash was only a few short blocks away.

They were visibly upset and needed someone to listen. As each one spoke and shared their feelings, their faces began to relax and I was amazed anew at the power of simply being heard.

I also met a woman that day who lived directly beside the crash. The mom of triplets, she was shaken by the tragedy's proximity to her home and grateful that her family had been spared. Still, her joy was dampened by the loss of dear neighbors. Even in the midst of devastation and destruction, I saw God in her face as she spoke of that loss with compassion and concern.

A fellow who lived in the house across the street from where the plane came down told me he had worked all night the evening before the crash and, being quite tired, had gone straight to bed. He said he had high hopes of snoozing through the afternoon. He was sleeping in his back bedroom when an awful explosion jarred him awake.

He had tried to leave his home through the front door but, finding the extreme heat far too intense, he had retreated to the rear of his house and fled. He, too, was awestruck and grateful to be alive.

Many of the homes in this neighborhood were occupied by firefighters, police officers and emergency personnel that were working at the World Trade Center crash site. They had already been traumatized by what they had seen and experienced there during recent months and now had fresh loss in their own backyards.

Fears ran high and many asked me, "When is this going to stop?"

I didn't have any easy answers for them. I could only listen and encourage them to keep pulling together and supporting one another. I was beginning to realize that people everywhere, even in the worst situations, can and will demonstrate love for their fellow person. I saw God in the hearts and hands of my New York brothers and sisters.

I confess that it was tough on the third morning when I was again assigned to the flight crash site so that blessings could be administered. The sight of those red bags was becoming more and more difficult for me and the grief they inspired in my depths was beginning to take its toll.

At that day's end, I requested a transfer and it was quickly granted. All of those who faced the heartache and suffering at that site understood the need for a change of scenery and duties. That evening, I prayed for those selfless and determined workers who would continue on, day after day, that they might find renewed strength and stamina for the sorrowful job at hand.

That evening, I fell asleep thinking of the story told to me by the fire captain after we had blessed the first red bag of remains.

The twin towers. A picture to remember. Lest we forget.

Picture of Father Chaplain Mychal Judge being carried
by rescue workers. "No greater love that a man lay down
his life for another." Father Mychal gave his life in the
line of duty for his love of others.

Construction workers removing debris
and searching for remains.

Commander Roland Kandle, Assistant Connie and Chaplain Ray.
Notice patches on board. These patches represent the many agencies
that were epresented at the WTC Disaster.

Christmas day in the Pit. Firefighter's of FDNY
and Chaplain Ed (left) and Chaplain Bob (right).
This is the day the chaplains met Mayor Giuliani.

The remains of the World Trade Center Towers
elevator system at the landfill.

This is the location where Captain Karin DeShore of the FDNY was when the first tower collapsed. She ran behind the big column and the other fireman ran through the window in the rear. See the silhouette.

Nino's is the restaurant that served as a respite area for all of the WTC workers. I believe this Nino's is now closed.

Chapter Eight

✝

Will to Survive: Captain Karin DeShore's Story

I retired on April 22, 2002, after 28 years of service as a captain with the New York City Fire Department Bureau of Emergency Medical Services. During my tenure, I responded to airplane crashes, train derailments, fires and any other type of request for emergency medical assistance in addition to participating in several multiple casualty incident disaster drills. However, nothing prepared me for Sept. 11, 2001. I reported to duty at 0500 hrs, at Battalion 6 in Elmhurst, Queens, New York. My lieutenant performed the patrol duties and I prepared myself for a day of administrative tasks. Sometime during the morning, an EMT advised me that a plane had struck the World Trade Center.

When I finally entered the lounge and saw it on the TV, I still did not believe it. I switched on my departmental radio to the city-wide frequency and listened as ambulance units were dispatched. Other units were asking for staging areas and the location of supervision. I immediately asked my lieutenant via radio to return to the battalion and within minutes we were en route to the World Trade Center with two additional emergency medical technicians. I notified the dispatcher of my response and was told to respond to the station area at West & Vesui (Westside Highway & Vesui Streets). When we approached the 59th Street bridge, the second plane struck. Cars were stopped, people were in the street with looks of total disbelief on their faces. After crossing the 59th bridge, we became part of a caravan of emergency vehicles speeding toward the WTC. Somehow we wound up at West & Vesui, where I met the chief who had taken charge of the ambulance units. I was placed under his command and my lieutenant was left with the ambulances and the keys as we started to walk with full equipment on stretchers south on the Westside Highway past both towers. Initially, I continuously encouraged the personnel to move further over to the right.

Debris kept falling down on us, but I was not prepared for what I saw when I looked up. Human beings, some on fire, some struggling, some either dead or resigned to their fate, were also coming down on us. My eyes followed one person to the ground – a sight that will remain with me forever. Then every few seconds, we could hear the sound of another person hitting the ground. By the time that we were at the southwest corner of the second building, near a pedestrian overpass, my encouraging words turned to orders, since more and more debris was coming down on us and cars were already on fire. The chief asked me for an ambulance crew to enter the tower with him and I was to wait for further instruction on the command frequency. I ordered two ladies to follow the chief with their equipment. I now became verbally aggressive and ordered everyone under the pedestrian overpass.

My back was turned toward the building when someone yelled, "It's blowing!" There was this immediate, indescribably loud noise, the ground starting shaking and I could feel what I call a force heading toward me. I never turned around. I ran maybe 10 feet when this force caught up with me. I threw myself behind the last support beam of the pedestrian crosswalk just as something red was going past me. Almost immediately, total darkness settled in. I was alone in the dark. The noise became unbearable and then a feeling of suffocation came over me. I kept repeating, "I don't want to die," over and over. Something hit my visor and I might have passed out. Next I remember an unbelievable silence. Suddenly, I heard a male voice asking over my right shoulder, "Is anybody out there?" I finally replied, "I am over here; please don't leave me." He said, "I can't see." I replied, "I can't see, either, but you talk and I'll talk and we'll find each other." I do not know who the man was, but we held onto each other, climbing over debris and bodies, but also picking up survivors. We were about eight or 10 people walking west. Everyone was covered with gray dust, supporting each other, while gasping for air, coughing, spitting, and vomiting.

The darkness turned to gray and I saw a row of houses to my right and a marina to my left. We entered a storefront shop, a distribution center for napkins and tablecloths for restaurants, and I utilized the napkins to bandage the wounded. I went outside with two police officers who tried unsuccessfully to start two boats in the marina, when I saw red and orange popping debris and heard these awful crashing sounds coming from the other tower. A decision was made to evacuate and to get as far away as possible. Two elderly females, one with a cane, and a male from the store came with us. The red area of explosions became wider and we feared another explosion. I do not think that anyone, including myself, had realized at that time that the other tower had collapsed. We walked as far as the water and I saw the outline of boats in the water, but none would come to our assistance. All of a sudden, this boat came into the marina, right up to the concrete where most of us were standing. I saw two officers in clean uniforms on the boat and asked them to evacuate all the wounded and elderly ladies. They never questioned my request. After everyone was loaded on the boat, I was still standing on the concrete, since I had not made up my mind what I was going to do next. Since my appearance apparently was so poor, I was not recognized as a woman and I was asked, "What the – are you going to do? Are you coming or not?" His next sentence made up my mind: "Blankity blank, it is coming at us!"

Once again, I heard this unbelievable sound. I jumped on the boat, closed the door with my left hand, and sank to my knees. We were immediately hit with debris. Darkness set in again and, once again, we all gasped for air, even inside the cabin. The two officers, one at the other door and one at the wheel, continued to talk like men about getting out of the marina. But the boat was tied up, which was a blessing, because it kept us from overturning. When the blasts were finally over, the boat was completely covered with debris and the windshield wipers did not work. The officer in the door untied the boat and told the other officer to 'just turn left; when you don't hit anything anymore, just keep going.' In the meantime, I went down into the cabin where a fireman, still attached to a board, was bleeding severely from the back. I had nothing to stop the bleeding, but we held hands and he said, "My name is Bob. Tell my wife I love her." I told him my name and we just held hands. I had to be physically carried off the boat and was subsequently transported to the Jersey City Medical Center for medical attention. A church bus, escorted by Jersey City police, returned me at 1100 hrs to my battalion where I found my husband sitting in my car. It was not until then that my husband, three daughters and six granddaughters found out that I survived the collapse of both towers.

It was not until six weeks later that I learned the identity of the officers that saved so many lives on 9/11. They were three New Jersey troopers that entered the marina without thinking of their own safety and were present when the second tower collapsed and then managed to guide the boat in total darkness and covered with debris out of the marina to safety. I and so many others will be forever indebted to them for their courage and dedication to their profession. I also needed to thank all employees and volunteers of the Jersey City Medical Center for their medical and emotional support and the countless other New Jersey citizens who came to our assistance.

While you have been patient to read my story, I would like for you to remember that it is only one story. We must remember that thousands were present, each with their own story. Many are no longer with us and their stories will never be told. Thank you again, New Jersey, especially my three heroes, and may God bless America!

Captain Karin DeShore

Chapter Nine

✟

Humor in a Place of Horror

As requested, I was next assigned to the World Trade Center site. I knew it would be difficult to return to the scene of such mass devastation, but my thoughts turned to Captain Karin and her own relentless duties at the 587 crash site. How did she face the stress, day after grueling day? As I lifted her up in prayer, I knew I would miss her but was relieved to be heading to another location.

My partner and I were told to circle the WTC site, offer assistance as needed, and be available if a Port Authority officer was recovered so we could perform a service for them. During our day, we came across many fire and police personnel and offered our listening. As they each relayed where they were and what they were doing at the time of the initial attack and eventual collapse, we were newly amazed by their collective courage and gifts to our country.

Then, as we about to move on, one firefighter told us he was having a really rough time handling what had happened. He then shared what seemed an unbelievable story. Somehow segments of his tale just didn't make sense and, to be candid, the outlandish adventure seemed just plain weird.

As I listened intently, it occurred to me that this fellow

was destined to have emotional problems later on. He was stretched out lengthwise with his feet crossed and his face was black with soot. Quite frankly, he looked like death warmed over.

As I approached him, he uttered softly, "I want something." It was difficult to hear him clearly, so I kneeled closer.

"I got'cha!" he shouted, jumping up and bursting into laughter with the other firefighters seated behind him at this rest site.

My partner and I laughed uproariously with them as we realized we'd been had. Yes, one might wonder, with so much devastation surrounding us, how humor could surface in such a place. It delighted us to discover that the very ones most entitled to feel depressed and despondent were showing effervescent spirit, playing practical jokes and making others laugh. Those who had suffered extreme trauma and severe loss were still offering hope and joy to others.

We are made in God's image and, when I looked at the mirth in the eyes of these men whose uniforms were covered with dust and whose shoulders had been sagging only moments before with fatigue, I knew He was among us.

They didn't have the luxury of requesting a change of pace or different venue. Instead, they showed up day after day, facing emotionally charged duties and getting a continually heartbreaking job done. The release they so desperately needed in order to keep going was achieved by injecting humor where few would dare.

After a good laugh with these brave and enduring men, I felt hopeful that my efforts and prayers could also go a long way in restoring cheer to hurting hearts (although I didn't plan to lay down on the ground and feign dementia).

You see, even in the most devastating times, love, humor and sacrifice can emerge from the most horrible places. These 16 acres of rubble were only the physical remains of a hateful deed. The one reality upon which the terrorists did not count was the spirit of Americans in response to devastation. It didn't occur to them that compassion and love could survive unspeakable tragedy and that God would prevail.

Hate has not only been turned to love, even in that dark and forbidding nest where evil struck, but also into the revelation that when circumstances seem unbearable, we give them to God. Nothing is impossible to God.

Chapter Ten
✝
A Special Favor

It was tough to believe that my final workday before leaving for home had arrived so swiftly. My time at Ground Hero, meeting families of victims and dedicated volunteers and heroic workers, had brought me a new perspective of everyone's experience there that reading the news or watching TV could never have fully conveyed.

When Commander Roland pulled me aside and asked me to personally escort a friend of his around the WTC area, I felt privileged and gratefully accepted. His friend's son had perished in the disaster and I was eager to contribute in any way possible to easing that family's pain.

As the man and his brother walked with me and another chaplain through the Pit, they repeatedly thanked the many firefighters, police officers and rescue workers for such honorable and relentless service.

At Fire Station Ten, a tall firefighter was standing outside and this father went over to him. Sharing that he had lost his son in the collapse and was grateful for all the work the firefighters and others had performed, the father gave a spontaneous hug to the man with whom he was speaking.

Reaching inside of his pocket, the firefighter tugged free an iron cross that had been cut from one of the beams of the World Trade Center towers. He gently placed it in the father's hand and told him he would keep working to find his son.

Everyone's eyes filled with tears at this exchange and, with hands shaking, the father and brother began to hug again those of us gathered near. It was an incredibly moving experience.

As we continued our walk down to the marina adjacent to the WTC site, he mused that this was the route his son had taken to work each day. Each morning, he had crossed on the ferry without incident – until that fateful morning two months earlier.

This grief-stricken dad continued on in silence as he absorbed the sights and sounds around us. He took a picture and asked me to pray.

Two hours soon passed and, as we neared the end of our tour, we paused and said a prayer at the towers. As we arrived back at our starting point at the site's west end, a worker who was washing the many trucks that contained debris, fragments of clothing and possibly remains of the victims came over and asked for a favor.

"This is a sacred place," he said solemnly, as he asked us to have a prayer. He said he felt in his heart that remains not discovered at the site would be in these trucks and he wanted to have them blessed.

Although I had never performed a blessing over a truck before, I asked the father if he would feel comfortable with my leaving for a moment. He said he would like to join us.

Together, we stood hand in hand and prayed openly for any remains that could be in these trucks, for their families and for the workers that were trying so diligently to locate them.

After finishing our prayer and saying our goodbyes, I noticed the change of expression on the father's face. It was unlike anything I had ever witnessed. When our tour together had begun, the grief and pain were apparent in his face. Now, as we prepared to leave, I saw nothing but peace and God's grace in his features. I knew I had experienced God Himself in this transformation. I was left with dual feelings of lingering sadness for that family's loss and joy that they left with newfound peace taking root.

When Commander Roland asked me to share the day's experiences with him, I shared all that had happened and was startled when he hugged me. He was very thankful that his friend had a chance to find some solace after his tragic loss.

Afterward, we debriefed about my experiences and observations. It was a bit tough for me to accept that it was already time to go home. There was still so much to be done and I was going to miss my visits in the field. I would miss the witness of the workers and especially being of service in such a personal and hands-on way. I wanted to stay, but knew I couldn't.

Seeing my evident sadness, Commander Roland simply said, "Don't worry; you'll be back."

He was wiser than I knew.

Chapter Eleven

✝

Home Is Where My Wife Is

Many years ago, I was asked by a friend to sing at his wedding and I complied. It wasn't particularly memorable for me, other than my being thrilled that he was happy and looking forward to good times ahead.

Unfortunately, those good times were spent with a woman other than the one in white that day. So, many years later, after they divorced, I met his early bride at a dance. I didn't realize the connection until she reminded me that she had been the one in white. We've been dancing together ever since and have been joyously married for two decades.

As I headed home after my emotionally exhausting time of service in New York City, I was overjoyed to see my bride, as well as my brother and his wife, waiting for me at the Amtrak station. It felt wonderful to see them and our reunion reminded me with fresh force that it is a blessing to have such a great family with whom to share my life. The loss felt by so many others had reminded me as little else could to be genuinely and profoundly grateful for those beside me.

Driving across Afton Mountain and into the Shenendoah Valley, I began to share my experiences with them. It seemed I couldn't stop talking about all of the people I had met and lives who'd touched mine. We stayed up past midnight and then I fell into an exhausted slumber.

The next morning, when I awoke, I made some coffee and, just for the briefest of moments, I reached for my boots to head to the Command Center where I would receive my daily assignment. I chuckled, acknowledging that my chief commander now was my wife, and expressed again my appreciation for her as we shared breakfast.

Life got back to normal but, then again – could it?

Though I tried to return to my typical routine, it was impossible to pretend that nothing had changed. Thanksgiving had arrived and, quite frankly, it was impossible for me to sit at the table eating turkey without thinking of the thousands of people who wouldn't be able to share such a meaningful meal with their lost loved ones.

Soon, the Christmas season, too, was upon us and still I had not felt right in my own shoes at home.

When the phone rang one afternoon and I learned that more volunteers were needed to return to New York, my breath caught. I was needed and knew I would return.

Still, when I asked when I was needed, the caller was silent. Wondering whether he hadn't heard me, I repeated my question.

"Volunteers are needed the week of Christmas," he said, slowly, as though he, too, was holding his breath.

That was not the answer I wanted to hear. Christmas was a tough time to leave – for many reasons. My wife and

I had gotten engaged on Christmas Eve 14 years earlier and I just didn't see how I could leave her again so soon.

Also, I had been the new pastor of my church, Mount Zion-Linville Church of the Brethren, for only two months when I first went to volunteer in New York. Should I agree to pitch in again, it would leave them with a pulpit to fill on extremely short notice.

To my astonishment, both Gail and our church were immediately supportive of my desire to return. The church congregation even collected a love offering to send along for sharing with whomever I might find in need during my second visit.

I was humbled by their selfless encouragement and truly saw God in their faith and love.

Time flew between that initial phone call from the International Conference of Police Chaplains asking me to return and my departure for New York. It seemed only days later I was again standing before Commander Roland in the Command Center. When he asked to see me privately in his office, I wondered why.

His news stunned me: Since he was taking a Christmas holiday break, he was leaving me in command of the center for three days.

Had I heard him right? I was shocked and, to be candid, felt a bit afraid of the responsibility, but I also felt immensely honored by his confidence in me. I knew, with the help of God and my fellow chaplains, we could do the job well.

Once he had filled me in on the necessary tasks and then notified the staff of his decision, he headed out and left me there to handle the rest of the business at hand.

After the staff and I had a little pep talk, where I confessed this position was new to me and we'd all have to pull together, I went back to the hotel and slept soundly.

A new adventure was about to begin.

Chapter Twelve
✝
Back to Work

I wanted to wake up, full of enthusiasm and leadership zeal, so I was dismayed when my first breath the next morning was followed by a rattling cough and growing awareness of the stuffiness in my head and tightness in my throat.

This was NOT the time for a respiratory infection.

Pulling myself out of bed, I struggled to begin the day with some semblance of organization. As the other volunteers and I gathered in the lobby, we discovered we were short of drivers. After a mad scramble to consolidate, we managed to get ourselves to the Command Center.

The situation did not improve upon our arrival and I quickly found out how difficult being in charge could be. The breakfast food, which had always been hot and delicious during my past tour, was cold on this morning. The radios we needed to use did not function, either, in our part of the building AND we only had one driver to get us all to our geographically diverse assignments.

I had the sudden realization that the next three days were going to be very challenging, indeed!

Fortunately, we all pulled together and everyone made it somehow to the various locations. That afternoon, I spent a couple of hours at the WTC site and was able to deliver handwritten letters from my congregation to firefighters, police personnel and other workers. It was gratifying to see their appreciation at these gestures of compassion and remembrance.

Each time I would share a note, the police officers and rescue workers would stop what they were doing and eagerly open the letters, reading them as I waited. Most responded with deep emotion, crying at the sentiments expressed inside. They were delighted to know that total strangers were thinking of them from afar and keeping them in their prayers.

One New York police officer shared with me that he had not only lost his fellow officers at the World Trade Center decimation, but his year had also held personal challenges with his father moving in and his sister becoming extremely ill. His winter had been a distressingly long one, with long hours in the bitter cold and tumultuous weather.

After my time with him in the Pit, my own worries had paled. What was a mere head cold in the face of this man's despairing experience? I was reminded of my own comparative fortune and felt gratified to be able to return to the company of so many helpful individuals.

My hope, as I returned to the Command Center ranks to organize the next shift, was for clear sinus passages but, to my dismay, it was evidently not yet time for my full recovery. I took another dose of medication and jumped back into the tasks at hand.

It looked like we would again be short of drivers the next day. Perhaps someone from the local police department could help us, though everyone's ranks were slim in this exhausted city – especially nearing the holiday's peak.

Our dinner was again cold and it occurred to me that, not only was the oven not working, but the volunteer ranks were slimming now that three months had passed since September's terrorist attacks.

Since it was Christmas Eve, not many restaurants were open. But we were eager for something appetizing and hot to eat and so we kept searching. Finally, a small restaurant promised to deliver some food to us. We were all grateful for the answer to our prayers.

It had been an extremely long day, and several of the chaplains expressed discouragement over the communication malfunctions and food shortage.

We continued to test our radios and searched for different locations in the building that would support our efforts to communicate. None could be found. We finally decided that we would have to go outside every two hours to use our radios and exchange information. This meant leaving the Command Center unmanned and brief gaps of time in which we could not be in constant contact with our teams at the sites. This predicament left me feeling extremely uneasy, but we had little choice.

We were all discouraged and the morning seemed far too near, so we closed the Command Center ahead of schedule and headed to our hotel to get some rest. Because my cold had escalated into a sinus infection, I slept upright on the couch while the other chaplains fell fast asleep in their beds.

I was miserable.

Still, before I nodded off to sleep, I looked around me at the extra blankets the chaplains had heaped around me for comfort and warmth and saw the medicine and additional pillows they had placed within easy reach.

Smiling, I knew God was in our midst and I thanked him once more for the gift of His son. Though it was tough to have missed spending our engagement anniversary with my wife and being away on this day, I knew somehow that this year's Christmas would be very special in its own unique way.

Chapter Thirteen

✟

New Jersey Policeman Bob Rice's Story

"When I was sent to New York on September 14th, 2001, it was to help fellow public-safety workers cope with the overwhelming horrors of Ground Zero. I never realized the impact the ministry of others counselors at the site would have on my life.

The first thing I was required to do upon arriving at Ground Zero was to tour the site. After all, I was told, it's impossible to talk about what's going on out there if you haven't seen it. I only lived 96 miles from New York City in New Jersey but, believe it or not, I had never been to the city.

What greeted me there was something I hope I never have to see again. My colleagues and I wandered around the site and its devastation for hours. Not only was the carnage overwhelming, but I was a bit out of my element since I was assigned to work with men called by God to serve as chaplains.

Sure, I was raised in a Catholic environment until I was 6 years old and, through the years, friends had tried to introduce me to their various religious beliefs. But I didn't have good experiences in any of those situations.

And if you could have heard my typical language when I first arrived at Ground Zero, you would've known it reflected my spiritual decay. I cursed non-stop. You would never have wanted to have a conversation with me. The words that came out of my mouth would scare a truck driver.

Then I met Chaplains Greg and Gary from California and Chaplain Ricky from Texas. They had each been invited to serve in New York through the International Conference of Police Chaplains. Two of them were southern Baptists and the other was a Calvary Chapel preacher.

Chaplain Gary and I would frequently walk the site and talk. He was listening to everything I said and every foul word that came out of my mouth. He told me I needed some substitution words for my language.

Little by little – and it definitely didn't come quickly – the foul language began to clean up – and so did my heart.

One of the first areas it occurred to me that I needed change in my life was the way I viewed women. Chaplain Gary was always noticing my head turning toward many of the attractive women who visited the site – even though I had a photo of my wife on the visor of my patrol car.

Chaplain Gary had a helpful suggestion.

"What is something that you don't like?" he asked me.

I told him, "Chicken McNuggets."

"Well, every time you look at those women, you should think of Chicken McNuggets," he suggested. "They are Chicken McNuggets and, at home, you have prime rib."

From that moment, something shifted for me and my glances at other women began to change.

One day, I was on break and looking for something to read. Chaplain Ron, another volunteer, gave me the New Testament book of John. Later, he asked me what I thought of what I'd read and I confessed that I didn't understand it.

Chaplain Ron told me that I needed the Lord to give me wisdom and power to understand it, so I asked him how He could do that.

Chaplain Ron explained, "Just talk to Him like you would a friend."

Later, I talked with Chaplain Gary about what I'd been told and he joked that, based on my earlier foul language, I might not want to talk to God like I did my friends. I laughed and we had a discussion about what it means to talk to God.

I started calling those chaplains "my three wise men." When it was time for them to leave, I was crying, Gary was crying and I had my wife on the phone and she was crying.

As Chaplain Gary was saying his final farewells, he asked me to tell Chaplain Ricky, the newly arrived chaplain, "to finish what I started." I wasn't sure what he meant, but I passed it on, anyway.

My heart was being drawn more and more toward God and spiritual things. Something was happening to me and I didn't know what it was. Finally, I went looking for Chaplain Ricky at Port Authority Headquarters in Jersey City and told him I needed to have the Lord Jesus in my life.

As I prayed to accept Christ as my personal Lord and Savior, we had no idea we'd accidentally autodialed Chaplain Greg on Ricky's cell phone. He was able to hear the entire conversation and prayer!

Since that day, I haven't looked back. I live out my

belief in God every day. At home, my family is forever changed. My son, Bobby, who is a teenager, was involved in alcohol and drugs and was at the point of moving out of our house. God has transformed his life just like He did mine. Bobby hasn't touched drugs or alcohol since accepting Christ.

The climax of God's work with my family so far was when my wife Kimberly, son Michael and I were baptized together. Our entire family is now enmeshed in the life of our local congregation in Bellmawr, New Jersey. We are there whenever the doors are open.

I'm still a member of the New Jersey Critical Incident Stress Management Team and now I'm known as the "Ranting Reverend" or "Reverend Bob" by my colleagues. Through the relationships I developed in the aftermath of 9/11, my life has been changed forever.

Bob Rice

Chapter Fourteen

✝

Oh Holy Day

There was no Santa Claus in the Pit and those of us who awoke to work there Christmas morning clung to thoughts of the sacred nativity and hope that restores all.

It was tough not to feel lonely as we each called our beloved family members and wished them a merry morning. My wife had been wholly loving and selfless in her decision to encourage my volunteerism, and I did my best to show her my absolute appreciation during our call. Still, I felt my Christmas was incomplete without her by my side.

Acknowledging our need to celebrate the holy day, the other chaplains and I agreed that we would divide the shifts so that everyone would serve only half a day.

My stint in the Pit began that afternoon with a chaplain from Oklahoma. He was a jolly fellow and loved to sing. Everywhere we went, he would burst into song, belting out "We wish you a merry Christmas" to whomever was there.

As we descended into the Pit area, he began to sing joyously to a group of firefighters. They lit up like Christmas trees and wide smiles spread across their faces. We launched into conversation, all sharing about our families. It felt wonderful to see happiness on their features and to feel our own joy inside.

A limousine was parked near the curb and we discovered Mayor Rudy Guiliani was visiting Ground Hero. I approached his entourage and our request for permission to meet the mayor was granted.

My partner started singing and I joined in. Everyone turned to look at us with surprise on their faces. Perhaps our a cappella singing was a bit off key.

We spotted the mayor and walked over to shake his hand, then wished him a merry Christmas and happy new year. He was shorter than I expected and, somehow, seeing that someone I respected so deeply was also diminutive in stature like me left me feeling taller.

After leaving the Pit, we made our way to Fire Station Ten., where I discovered the firefighter in charge was someone I'd first met in November. He jubilantly shared that his assignment was complete and he was heading home at week's end. His time there had been tough, as it was his job to search day after day for victims, including his own friends and co-workers, and then record the information. It was an anguishing and relentless task and his rest would be well deserved.

It was my privilege, later, to escort a young girl and her family to the North Tower pit. Her brother had died during its collapse and they wanted to toss in some flowers as remembrance. With permission, they gathered to pay homage with prayer, their grief and heartache clear. Once they had dropped the flowers into the cavernous hole, they became calm and introspective.

This Christmas Day was particularly moving because many volunteers and workers were still giving their time, on this holiest of days, to seek the remains of victims. It takes extreme mental and physical endurance to pursue such a task, literally digging and scraping in the hope of finding some shred of identity that will bring peace to mourning families.

Throughout the day and into the night, my hearty companion continued to sing his way into the hearts of those we passed. It was truly Christmas in his heart and I couldn't help but feel merrier because of him.

Our mutual goal that day had been to touch at least one life in an encouraging and uplifting way. As we looked back, we recognized clearly that others had, in fact, touched us in many, many forms – what a powerful Christmas gift we had each received!

In each person we had met, I saw God in His many forms – permitting us to feel grief, hope, joy, despair, celebration, tribute, love and comfort. I had been blessed again and again.

It was a Christmas Day celebration I would never forget.

Chapter Fifteen
✟
More Work To Do

Once Christmas Day has passed, Commander Roland returned to resume his duties. I must admit that I was a little more than a bit relieved!

Assigned with another chaplain to the morgue at Belleview Hospital, we were on hand to perform services for any fallen officers whose remains were unearthed.

Each time a transport vehicle arrived, we all stood in line and paid our respects as the remains were taken from the ambulance. It was quite moving to salute the fallen heroes and my heart pounded with emotion at their sacrifice. As the medical examiner searched for personal identification or identifying characteristics, we stood near, waiting until DNA samples had been gathered and the remains placed respectfully in refrigerated trailers.

For those who faced these rituals daily, it was an emotionally charged workday. The sights were gruesome and the odor penetrating. It was unforgettable.

When identification was possible, we performed a service and then the remains were transferred to a funeral home. It was satisfying to know that somewhere a family could find a bit of solace in placing their loved one at rest.

As the day advanced, our assignment was extended

to other areas and we made our way through Ground Hero, Fire Station Ten and St. Paul's Church. At the barricade, throngs of people were gathered and, after we related the discovery of several firefighters' bodies, they launched into thunderous applause. It was indescribably emotional and I fought back a cascade of tears.

I saw God all around me – not just in the faces of the people that served directly at this disaster scene, but in the hearts of the ones who demonstrated so much concern for those giving their all at the site and the precious remains they recovered. It was very humbling.

Throughout that day and the next, when I was again assigned to the morgue, I was continually reminded of the selfless nature of so many around me and the valor of those who had given their lives. It was an overwhelming privilege to be present to offer blessings as so many courageous souls were laid to rest.

Again I was nearing the end of my tour of duty and, once more, I was feeling mixed emotions about leaving. It would be great to celebrate a belated Christmas with my family, as well as finally give my weakened body a break, but I also wanted to stay and continue to encourage those around me who so desperately needed comfort.

What I had experienced at Ground Hero had changed me in ways I could not yet fully define and I thanked God for showing me anew that He is all around us – always – in every circumstance. We are never alone and we are always, always loved.

My final day as a volunteer there included a new view – I was assigned to the landfill. The depository of all the truckloads of material from the Trade Center site itself, it contained the dust and metal from the buildings, as well as likely remnants of victims killed when the planes hit.

Once I was suited up in white overalls, booties, gloves, a helmet with goggles and a respirator – imagine the Michelin man in outer space – we toured the grounds.

To say the magnitude of what they sought to achieve at this site was astounding is an understatement. One area was devoted to pieces of elevator. In another, workers were painstakingly sifting through all of the piles of dust and debris that had been brought in from the Pit. Even the smallest particle could be used to identify lost individuals and it was nearly incomprehensible to understand the patience required for this task.

Every minute particle was inspected, identified and labeled.

Another section stored hundreds of destroyed vehicles. It was an incredible sight. Piles of crushed cars, trucks, fire equipment, police cruisers and other unidentifiable heaps were strewn over many acres. The force of the buildings collapsing had crushed these vehicles like they were matchboxes.

During our time together, my guide confided that he felt empty inside – not only because of the intense nature of his job, but because he felt unappreciated. Most of the world's attention was on the WTC site and few recognized the emotionally supercharged environment and intense dedication of those at this landfill. It was behind the scenes and seemingly forgotten.

His honesty was refreshing and, even as I assured him that God would bless them for their efforts, I vowed to share with others what I had seen so that their light, too, could shine. Sometimes a little encouragement is all it takes for someone to find renewed spirit to continue despite daunting demands.

As we prepared to leave, our guide gave me the helmet I had worn as a gift. He had signed it as a keepsake, knowing I would treasure any fragments of my time in New York.

That evening, I gathered with those with whom I had spent so much time volunteering and serving others. We had become a bit of a family and it was tough to know that our time together was ending.

I saw God in each of their expressions as we laughed and cried together, knowing our experiences from these past weeks had become part of our shared history, bonding us in a way nothing else could ever achieve.

I was grateful and sad and tired and satisfied. I was ready to go home.

Chapter Sixteen
✠
I Saw God

My life purpose is to inspire and empower others to have a vision of God's love and joy in their lives. I want to walk humbly and serve playfully, passionately, prayerfully and powerfully to encourage others to do the same.

I have always believed in honesty and integrity. I love to laugh and cry as well. Truly, I love life and enjoy it every day. Injustice saddens me, yet I know God is in control.

I am excited about the future – yet am content to live one day at a time. I believe we have been brought together for divine purpose and I know God is going to do whatever it takes to have His glory realized. I want to be part of that.

I look forward to life and I will live each day to serve others and, at the same time, take care of my family. I have been blessed and it all belongs to God.

I believe we all have a destiny and that God has a plan for each of us. He is using me and I am humbled, blessed and utterly amazed at what He has done in my life. He took this short little fellow, who kind of resembles the Pillsbury dough boy, and has shaped me into a pastor and one of His instruments of love. What more can a person ask for?

My faith in God is real. It has been tested, mind you – there are times when I feel all the water in the well has dried up and I could use a hug from God. But, sometimes, getting to the bottom of the water tests our faith and inspires us to really trust God. I confess that I'm a feeling kind of guy and, sometimes, I don't feel Him around me – yet I can always know He is there. I always know that the Holy Spirit will guide me through life, no matter the page.

My time in New York after 9/11 was no exception.

What I saw there and experienced tested my emotional and physical stamina. There were days when I wanted to quit – I was sick and I was exhausted and I missed the comforts of home and cheerful company of my bride.

God nudged me in those moments and showed me the fortitude and heart of those around me who were stepping beyond their own physical needs to vigorously pursue comfort and consolation for others. He never failed to inspire me through their example and I will forever consider myself privileged to have worked among them.

Whether it was the Pit where so many had died, the airport that held fresh destruction, the morgue and its solemn purpose or the landfill and its overwhelming accumulation of debris and decay, God was in the midst, bringing hope and inspiration where none could otherwise exist.

He was in the bosom of every person who so unselfishly devoted their lives, time and effort to rescue, feed, clothe, counsel, debrief, identify and bury others. Ground Hero had many warriors in its depths and they served valiantly.

When the first plane – and then the second – hit the World Trade Center towers, God was there, grieving evil and lifting up those who were taken from our world too soon. He filled the hearts and bodies of those left behind with the necessary strength and will to continue despite unspeakable loss.

I saw God firsthand in the words, actions and very faces of the people I met in New York. As a result of their selfless efforts and compassionate actions, my faith in Him has been deepened.

My sincere prayer is that, as you face life's circumstances and the challenges they bring, you, too, will open your heart to a God who loves you.

He is with each of us – always – if only we accept His gift of love.

✝

About the Author

Bob Johnson is the pastor of the Blue Ridge Chapel Church of the Brethren in Waynesboro, Virginia. Chaplain Bob is a Master Chaplain with the International Conference of Police Chaplains (ICPC), where he currently serves as a disaster response team member and holds life membership. He also serves as the Mid-East Regional Director for the organization, providing administrative leadership for chaplains in seven states and the Washington D.C. area.

Chaplain Bob served two tours of duty at the World

Trade Center disaster site in New York. He recently served as the point man for the ICPC in Gulfport, Mississippi, in the aftermath of Hurricane Katrina, serving the police departments of Gulfport, Long Beach, and Pass Christian.

Chaplain Bob has just finished the National Incident Management Training from FEMA as part of the Homeland Security disaster response team and is also a member of the Blue Ridge Critical Incident Stress Team. In addition to his service in law enforcement chaplaincy, he also serves as a volunteer Chaplain at Augusta Medical Center, where is also a member of the chaplain's supervisory committee.

Chaplain Bob has served as a Chaplain for the Staunton-Augusta Rescue Squad, the Staunton Police Department and is now serving as Chaplain for the Waynesboro Police Department. He is a former FBI chaplain who served in Washington D.C. He is a life member of the Staunton-Augusta Rescue Squad and served as a sergeant of a patrol unit with the Staunton Police Reserves.

He has written a training seminar, called *The Ministry of Presence: One-on-One*, and is currently developing a training book on this program. Bob has presented this seminar at the International Annual Training Conference of the ICPC and at regional training seminars as well. He has spoken at the Virginia Occupational Safety and Health annual conference on his experiences at the WTC disaster site and has shared his story with many local civic organizations as well.

Bob is supported by his lovely wife, Linda Gail Johnson. She is Augusta Medical Center's executive director of the AHC Community Health Foundation and the Director of the Community Wellness Department. Her encouragement and moral support have been invaluable.

After trying his hand at scuba diving and flying, Bob's more conservative hobbies include horses, mini-farming, fishing and singing barbershop and gospel music. He feels called to teach and loves to provide renewal and revival programs for Christian faith groups of all denominations.

His perfect retirement plan includes an RV with a ministry that travels wherever God leads.

✝
Power of Presence

We would all be amazed at how our presence affects others. When we walk in a room after our company has arrived or, when you arrive at work and enter your work space, look at the reaction of those around you. What do you imagine they are thinking? What does your presence mean to them? Is it positive or not so positive? Your aura leaves a lasting impression on those who meet and greet you.

As a chaplain, I have found just by walking into a situation, those who see you believe you represent a higher power. You don't have to say or do anything. They recognize that you are someone they can talk to and trust. I have been told many times that I represent God to them. They would say, "You are a man of God." That is a lot of responsibility to lay on one's shoulders, but I take that responsibility very seriously.

What would your reaction be if you walked up to a New York Police officer and he started to express his heartwrenching feelings about the WTC disaster and his personal experience to you? This happened to me - I listened; he spoke. When he was done, he handed me his NYPD tie clip and said, "Thank you for listening." I simply said, "You are welcome" and left.

The question here is did my presence make a difference? Does yours? People are looking for those who are willing to listen and encourage them. They are looking for someone to care. When we serve others by giving of ourselves, our presence will always make an everlasting impression and difference in other lives.

Do you fit that description?

I have long dreamed of writing a second book about the power of presence and, at last, that wish has come true and is currently in production. It is my wish that "The Power of Presence" will enhance the training seminar I have also completed about the ministry of presence.

Thank you for your trust in buying "I Saw God." If you would like someone to come and speak on this subject, the power of presence or do a renewal service, I would be honored. Feel free to contact me through Bob Johnson Ministries.

In His love,
Chaplain Bob Johnson
Pastor